ABUNDANT BLESSINGS
To Dad, with Love

By Debbie Violette
Illustrated by Katherine Messenger

Editor: Amy Ashby

ISBN: 978-1-7350915-1-8 (hard cover)
      978-1-7350915-2-5 (soft cover)

Published by Warren Publishing
Charlotte, NC
www.warrenpublishing.net
Printed in the United States

For my dad, John,
for teaching me to have faith, pray, and
open my heart. You will always be one
of my greatest blessings and I am so
grateful for you. I love you forever.

Author's Note

On May 2, 2000, my dad, John, who had been healthy his entire life, was diagnosed with prostate cancer. My whole world came crashing down at the thought of losing him. I come from a large family of nine kids and our dad instilled in each of us the importance of loyalty, hard work, faith, and family. He taught us the true meaning of unconditional love and he, along with our loving mother, was always there for us no matter what. He had always been my rock, my inspiration, my spiritual leader, and my everything. I wrote this poem for him and brought it to the hospital the day of his prostate surgery. These words came straight from my heart. Thankfully, my dad made a full recovery and it is such a blessing that he is still with us today.

I truly hope this book will help you to reflect upon and pay tribute to those extraordinary men in your life. I have included a section in the back for you to write your own thoughts and feelings to the special man who may receive this book as a gift. I do hope you take advantage of those blank pages and fill them up with words of love, thankfulness, and hope. Sometimes it is easier to write down our deepest thoughts and feelings than to say them out loud. Or if you happen to be going through a time of sadness or loss, I hope these words will provide you with some comfort and peace as you reflect upon happy memories.

Abundant blessings to you and yours!

With love,
Debbie Violette

You are my pillar of strength,
the shield that protects me
when all else fails,

the ear to listen,

the heart that loves.

Your guidance has never failed me,
to you I owe so much.

Your strong, silent, yet gentle ways
have brought me comfort and peace
in an uncertain world.

The hope you give me lifts me up always.

The faith you have instilled in me never fails.

I know you are always by my side,
quietly, even when I am alone.

To you, I owe so many things ...
the gleam in my eyes,

the smile on my face,

the spirit in my personality.

You have taught me to love openly,
to give freely to other people,

to always be kind,
to be happy with who I am,
and to see who I am yet to become.

I love you, my dear father,
and I thank you for your gentle ways.

You have given me more than
you will ever know.

NOTES TO DAD

Notes to Dad

CPSIA information can be obtained
at www.ICGtesting.com
Printed in the USA
BVHW022246290620
582543BV00014B/324